PLANET UNDER PRESSURE
FOOD

Paul Mason

Heinemann Library
Chicago, Illinois

© 2006 Heinemann Library
a division of Reed Elsevier, Inc.
Chicago, Illinois

Customer Service 888-454-2279

Visit our website at
www.heinemannraintree.com

Editorial: Sarah Shannon
and Louise Galpine
Design: Lucy Owen and Bridge
Creative Services Ltd
Picture Research: Natalie Gray
and Sally Cole
Production: Chloe Bloom

Printed and bound in China by South China
Printing Company

10 09 08 07 06
10 9 8 7 6 5 4 3 2 1

Library of Congress Cataloging-in-Publication Data

Mason, Paul, 1967-
  Food / Paul Mason.
    p. cm. -- (Planet under pressure)
  Includes bibliographical references and
index.
  ISBN 1-4034-7746-9 (library binding-
hardcover : alk. paper)
  1. Nutrition policy. 2. Food supply. I. Title.
II. Series.
  TX359.M37 2006
  363.8--dc22

2005017062

Acknowledgments
The publishers would like to thank the
following for permission to reproduce
copyright material: Alamy pp. **6–7** (John
Angerson), **8–9** (Pat Behnke), **40–41** (Nick
Spurling); Alamy/Imagestate pp. **32–33**;
Corbis pp. **18–19**; Corbis pp. **16–17**; (Steve
Rayner), **20–21** (Matthew Mcvay), **24–25**
(Keren Su), **28–29** (Marc Granger), **30–31**
(Michael Lewis); Corbis/Bettmann pp. **14–15**;
Cumulus pp. **24–25**; Fair Trade pp. **34–35**;
Getty pp. **28–29** (Judith Hæusler); Panos pp.
6–7 (Sven Torfinn), **10–11** (Mark Henley),
38–39 (Chris de Bode); Roslin Institute pp.
36–37; Still Pictures pp. **4–5** (Mark Edwards),
10–11 (Alex S Maclean), **26–27** (Mark
Edwards), **34–35** (Dylan Garcia), **38–39** (Nick
Cobbing); TopFoto pp. **12–13**;
TopFoto/Images Works pp. **22–23**; Trip pp.
36–37 (R Drury).

Cover photographs of soldier handing out
food and of woman in supermarket
reproduced with kind permission of Corbis.

Every effort has been made to contact
copyright holders of any material
reproduced in this book. Any omissions
will be rectified in subsequent
printings if notice is given to the publishers.

The paper used to print this book comes
from sustainable resources.

Dedicated to the memory of Lucy Owen

Contents

Any words appearing in the text in bold,
like this, are explained in the Glossary.

Food Issues Around the World

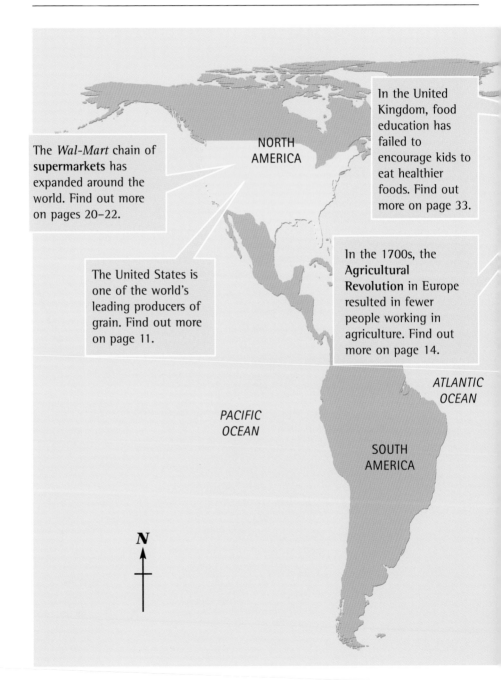

The *Wal-Mart* chain of **supermarkets** has expanded around the world. Find out more on pages 20–22.

NORTH AMERICA

In the United Kingdom, food education has failed to encourage kids to eat healthier foods. Find out more on page 33.

The United States is one of the world's leading producers of grain. Find out more on page 11.

In the 1700s, the **Agricultural Revolution** in Europe resulted in fewer people working in agriculture. Find out more on page 14.

ATLANTIC OCEAN

PACIFIC OCEAN

SOUTH AMERICA

N

In the United Kingdom, roughly 75 percent of the population is overweight; in 2003, 22 percent were **obese** (so overweight that it affected their health). Find out more on page 7.

Golden Rice is a **genetically modified** crop. Find out more on page 25.

Over recent years, China has managed to feed its people better, despite a growing population. Find out more on page 9.

EUROPE

ASIA

Bread often contains fat and other additives. Find out more on page 41.

In Khalipathar, Orissa, India, almost one third of the population does not have enough to eat. Read more on page 10.

AFRICA

Kenya exports vegetables and other foods, but vegetable consumption among Kenyans has decreased. Find out more on page 31.

INDIAN
OCEAN

AUSTRALIA

Feeding the World

Food and water provide the energy our bodies need to function; without it our bodies become weak and susceptible to disease. Eating and drinking less than our bodies require leads to starvation and eventually death. Depending on how much body fat we have, it can take up to 70 days without food to starve to death. The process is much quicker without water because a person cannot survive once his or her body has lost 20 percent of its water content.

Dying for a meal

More than ten million people die each year due to lack of food. In addition, almost two billion—or one third—of the people in the world suffer from **under-nutrition**: they are not getting enough to eat. This might make you think that there is not enough food to go around, but in fact there is plenty. If all the cereal crops produced each year were divided equally among the world's population, everyone would have enough food.

An unequal world

The world's food is not shared equally. In 1997, for example, people in the United States ate an average of 3,699 **calories** a day; in Portugal, 3,667; in South Korea they ate 3,155. In other parts of the world, people were eating far less. In Haiti people ate 1,869 calories a day; in North Korea, 1,837; in Burundi, 1,685. These figures are averages; some people had less to eat, others had far more.

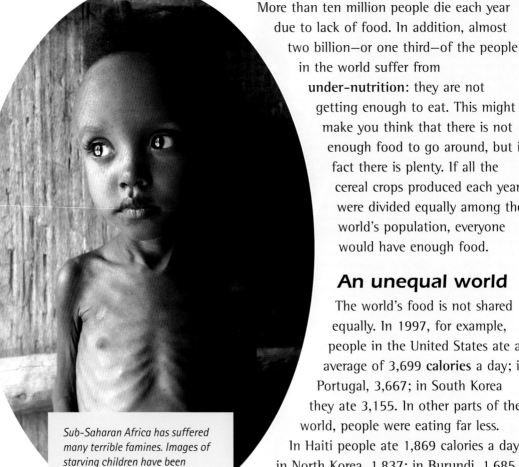

Sub-Saharan Africa has suffered many terrible famines. Images of starving children have been broadcast around the world, prompting massive aid efforts.

An unhealthy diet and lack of exercise have led to an increase in cases of obesity in developed countries.

Expanding waistlines

In some parts of the world, too much food—not too little—causes problems. More and more people are obese—overweight to the point where they are at risk from serious illnesses. This is mainly a problem in wealthy countries, where an average of 20.4 percent of people were obese in 1999. In poorer countries, only 1.8 percent of people were obese. However, increasing numbers of people in developing countries are also beginning to suffer obesity-related problems.

By 2004, obesity in the United States began to get out of control. That same year, a respected British health **watchdog** warned that obesity in the United Kingdom had grown 400 percent in 25 years. In the worst possible outcome, "children will die before their parents [because] of childhood obesity." Other likely effects of the rise in obesity include:

- more **diabetes**
- increased rates of cancer and heart disease.

What you can do to avoid obesity

- Eat fruit as a snack, instead of sweets
- Drink water, not carbonated beverages
- Do at least 30 minutes of exercise, 5 times a week.

Why we need food

The food we eat does several jobs. Food contains **nutrients** that provide materials for building, repairing, and maintaining body tissues. Nutrients help regulate our body processes and also serve as fuel to provide energy. Without this energy the body cannot maintain all its functions, such as breathing or movement.

ELEMENTS IN FOOD

Each day the human body needs each of these different elements found in food:

- **proteins**, which the body uses to grow and stay healthy
- **carbohydrates**, which provide the body with most of the energy it needs
- **fats**, which are an essential part of the body's makeup, and provide a concentrated source of energy.

People also need certain **vitamins** and **minerals** in their diet as well as water. If people do not get enough of each different type of food, they are said to be **malnourished**.

FOOD INTAKE

The energy in the food we eat is measured in **calories**. The more energy you use—by running around or working, for example—the more calories you need. On average men need 2,500 calories a day and women need 2,000 for their bodies to remain healthy. If people eat more than these amounts, they will gain weight; if they eat less, their body will not be able to function properly. People who do not get enough food to eat over a period of time become **undernourished**.

EFFECTS OF UNDERNOURISHMENT

If the body does not have enough nourishment, it becomes less able to fight off disease than would normally be the case. Many people who die each year for food-related reasons are killed by ordinary diseases that a well-fed person would be able to survive.

AN EXPANDING POPULATION

The world's population growth is fastest in the areas where some governments are already struggling to feed their citizens: Latin America, Africa, and South and Southeast Asia. Overall, the world's population is predicted to grow from 6.1 billion in 2001 to at least 9 billion in 2050. Providing food for all these extra mouths is one of the world's great future challenges.

China has improved the standard of living for its people despite rapid population growth. In 1949, average life expectancy was 35 years; today it is 71.4 years. China's government has done this partly by trying to limit population growth so that food production could keep pace with the expansion of the country's population.

Predicted growth in the world's population

2050 population
(9 billion
or 147 percent
bigger than today)

2025 population
(7.7 billion or
126 percent bigger
than today)

2015 population
(7.1 billion or
116 percent bigger
than today)

2005 population
more than 6.1 billion

How is our food produced?

Around the world, food is produced in a variety of ways. At one extreme, farmers in poor countries, such as Bangladesh, Senegal, or Guatemala, may work a small piece of land using simple tools, in what is called **subsistence** farming. In a bad year, they may not even grow enough to feed their family. At the other extreme are giant, high-tech farms in places such as Canada, the United States, and Australia, where vast amounts of food are produced for international sale.

Life in Khalipathar, India

Chudamani Nag is eleven years old and lives in Khalipathar, a village in the state of Orissa, India. During the summer, the village's fields grow rice, chili peppers, mangoes, limes, and eggplant. The animals include cows, buffalo, chickens, and goats. Despite this, 30 percent of the people, including Chudamani and his family, do not have enough to eat.

There is not enough food or work for everyone in Khalipathar. When the situation is at its worst, Chudamani and his family, along with half the village, head for Andhra Pradesh. For the next six months everyone, including the children, works in brick kilns making bricks. Wages are low, but it is the only work available to many of the villagers. The poorest, landless workers are the ones who have to leave their homes. The wealthier farmers, who own their own land, are able to grow and sell extra crops to make money, which helps them survive through the winter.

DIFFERENCES IN PRODUCTION

Regions where the amount of food we produce is highest are often those where the population is growing by the smallest amount. In the 24 years between 1975 and 1999, cereal crop production in Western Europe increased by 70 percent. But in 2000, the populations of Western Europe and North America were increasing by less than 1 percent each year.

In Africa, meanwhile, the population was increasing by 2 to 3 percent each year, but cereal crops had increased by just 15 percent in the 25 years from 1975. This means that there is not enough food being grown in the places that need it most.

Grain in the United States

North America is the number one grain-producing region in the world, growing 1.27 tons (1,156 kilograms) of grain per person. Farming in the United States and Canada is highly **mechanized**, with at least one tractor for every person working in agriculture. Ethiopia, by contrast, has fewer than five tractors for every 1,000 people who work in agriculture.

Grain farms in the United States and Canada can stretch for many miles. Mechanization means one farmer can cultivate huge areas of land.

The Food Industry

Growth of the food industry

Until about 12,000 years ago, humans lived by moving around, hunting wild animals, and gathering plants to eat. Then small groups of people began to settle close to reliable sources of food. Roughly 11,000 years ago, people in the Middle East began to grow their own food. These were the first farmers.

Several thousand years later, descendants of the first farmers were partly responsible for the appearance of the first cities. Because the farmers were able to grow more food than they needed for themselves, they had some left over to sell. This meant that other people had no need to grow or gather their own food. Instead, they could live in cities doing other work, and buy their food at the market. From 8000 to 3500 B.C.E., cities began to spring up around the world.

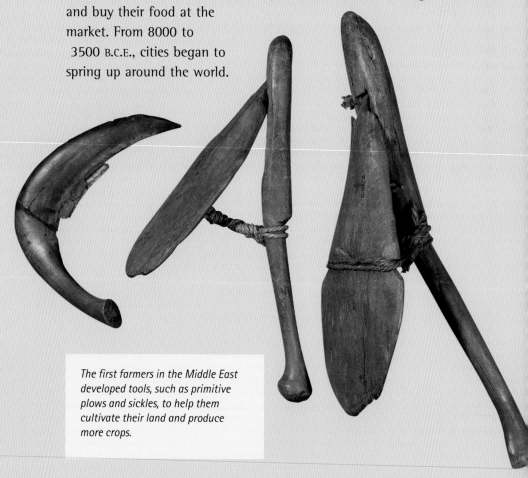

The first farmers in the Middle East developed tools, such as primitive plows and sickles, to help them cultivate their land and produce more crops.

Technology and food production

Technology—the tools, machines, and processes humans use to help them do jobs—played a crucial role in the development of the food industry. The first farmers learned how to use simple **irrigation** systems to grow more crops. Many of the world's first great civilizations grew up in river valleys for this reason. Societies emerged in areas such as the Nile valley of Egypt, the Tigris-Euphrates valley of Mesopotamia, the Indus valley of Pakistan and northwest India, and the Huang He valley of China.

THE AGRICULTURAL REVOLUTION

The Agricultural Revolution began in England in the early 1700s. By the end of the 1800s, it had spread across Europe and North America. Farmers began to use a variety of new techniques and machines. They started to rotate crops (see below), which allowed them to grow food on all their land and to keep animals for meat all year. New varieties of animal were bred, such as the Leicester sheep, which fattened far more quickly than other kinds of sheep and could therefore be sold at the market sooner. Inventions such as Jethro Tull's **seed drill** and Eli Whitney's **cotton gin** also allowed farmers to make more profit using fewer workers.

"Turnip" Townshend's big idea

In the early 1700s, Charles "Turnip" Townshend developed a way of using all his farmland each year. Townshend grew four crops, often turnips (his nickname), alfalfa, and two different types of wheat. By growing different crops in the same field each year, he made sure the soil had time to regain lost nutrients before the original crop was planted in it again. This simple idea, called crop rotation, could increase farmers' profits tremendously.

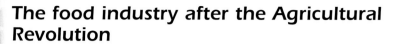

The food industry after the Agricultural Revolution

The Agricultural Revolution meant that by the 1800s, fewer people were needed to work in agriculture. Many farming people moved to the rapidly growing cities. The new factories offered jobs, though the conditions were often dangerous and the pay was poor. European and North American cities grew rapidly during this time. Fewer and fewer people actually grew the food they ate. Instead, they were increasingly dependent on the food industry to transport food to where it was needed.

By the 1800s, the food industry could transport goods over long distances. Using fast ships, new railways, and other technological developments, it was even possible for food to be taken from one country to another to be sold.

The food industry after World War II

After World War II, the food industry in wealthy countries began to change rapidly. Every few years, new technology allowed farmers to produce larger amounts of food. Farms became heavily mechanized. **Arable** farmers began to use **fertilizers** to help their crops grow bigger and faster. **Pesticides** reduced the amount of crop lost. Livestock farmers began to use factory-farming methods: large numbers of animals were kept in small spaces and fed until they were large enough to be slaughtered.

In the 1800s food began to be transported around the world by ship. Once meat was packed in ice, it could be shipped across oceans and still be fresh enough to eat when it reached port, thousands of miles away.

Today's world is becoming increasingly **urbanized**. More and more people live in towns and cities. Already nearly half the world's population lives in cities; by 2030 it will be 60 percent. This growth of cities has important implications for food supply around the world:

- Fewer people are able to feed themselves using food they have grown. The food industry has to expand in order to feed the city dwellers.
- To increase its output, the food industry must either grow more food on the same amount of land or use more land for food production. However, the expansion of cities is eating up agricultural land, meaning that less land is available, not more.

The world's largest cities

New York
Los Angeles
Mexico City
Istanbul
Beijing
Tokyo
Tianjin
Osaka
Cairo
Delhi
Karachi
Shanghai
Dhaka
Mumbai
Kolkata
Manila
Lagos
Jakarta
Rio de Janeiro
São Paulo
Buenos Aires

- Cities with a population of over 10 million in 2000
- Cities forecast to have a population of over 10 million by 2015

Food transportation today

In the past, when there were few ways to store fresh food, the type of food on people's tables depended largely on the time of year. In the summer, they might have strawberries, lettuce, or fresh meat. By the end of winter, only foods that could be stored were available, such as cheese, salted meat, potatoes, or wrinkled old apples. In the world's poorer countries, this is still the case, but in richer countries, the situation is now very different.

UNSEASONAL EATING

Just as farming became more **efficient** after World War II, so too did the transportation of food. Better packaging, refrigerated transportation containers, and faster trucks, trains, and aircraft were all developed. By the end of the twentieth century, it was possible to sit in a restaurant in Paris and eat fresh lobster from Maine and tomatoes from South Africa. In wealthy countries, most people today expect to be able to buy strawberries all year. In June the fruit might come from southern England, in December from Israel.

Produce is packed in sacks prior to transportation by air around the world.

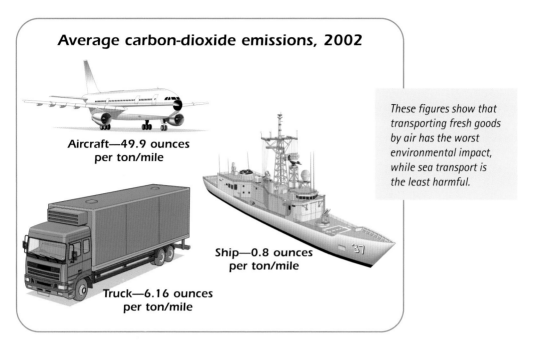

Average carbon-dioxide emissions, 2002

Aircraft—49.9 ounces per ton/mile

Ship—0.8 ounces per ton/mile

Truck—6.16 ounces per ton/mile

These figures show that transporting fresh goods by air has the worst environmental impact, while sea transport is the least harmful.

Costs of global food transport

The cost of transporting food around the world has been getting cheaper for several years. Between 1980 and 2000, the cost of sending food by sea fell by more than 70 percent. In the late 1990s, the cost of air transportation fell by 3 to 4 percent each year. However, there are additional, non-financial costs involved. The movement of food around the world has a significant effect on the world's **environment** and people's health.

Transportation of goods for trade is one of the fastest-growing sources of **greenhouse gases**. The pollution costs of moving food can be very high. Flying just 1.1 pounds (0.5 kilograms) of asparagus from Chile to New York releases 4.4 pounds (2 kilograms) of carbon dioxide into the atmosphere.

SPREAD OF DISEASE

Moving foods, including live animals, over long distances also makes it more difficult to control the spread of disease. A number of diseases, such as mad-cow disease, have been spread through the food transportation system.

FOOD SHORTAGES

Airplanes use a lot of fuel. International food supply by airplanes depends on fuel prices remaining relatively low. If prices suddenly increased, food transportation could become too expensive. This could lead to shortages of food in countries that receive a lot of their food supplies by air.

Food Giants

Today the food industry is a global, highly profitable business. It is dominated by relatively few very large companies that have a far-reaching influence on how food is supplied and sold in the West. In 2001, the French supermarket chain Carrefour, for example, sold $85.4 billion of food—more than twice as much as its rival, Tesco (a UK company). In the United States, the Kroger group earned more than $50 billion in food sales that same year.

Supermarkets have been criticized for taking an increasingly large share of the money people spend on food. In 1970, the average weekly sales in U.S. supermarkets were $44,000. By the late 1990s, they had reached $285,000. During the same period, smaller local food sellers in Europe were being driven out of business, unable to compete with the prices and convenience offered by the bigger stores.

Giant supermarkets are constantly trying to lower food prices to gain customers. The produce growers are then left with a smaller income.

Giant supermarket groups dominate the sale of food in wealthy countries. Because they sell so much of the food people buy, food producers, processors, and transporters can find it difficult to make a living unless they work with one of the giant chains.

Because the supermarkets are interested in driving prices down to the lowest possible level, it is difficult for farmers and others in the food-supply chain to get a good price for the food they produce. In 2000, only 22 cents of every dollar spent on food in the United States went to the people who produced the food. In 1996, $207 billion was spent on food in the United Kingdom: 35 percent of this went as profit to the sellers, with much of this going to the supermarket chains.

EFFICIENT CONSUMER RESPONSE

Almost all supermarkets operate what is called Efficient **Consumer** Response (ECS). This means that they do not store large stocks of food. Instead, they use barcodes and computerized ordering systems to reorder relatively small amounts when they are close to running out. This can cause difficulties for suppliers. They have to grow or raise enough food to be ready to fill large orders—but if only small orders arrive, farmers may struggle to sell their produce.

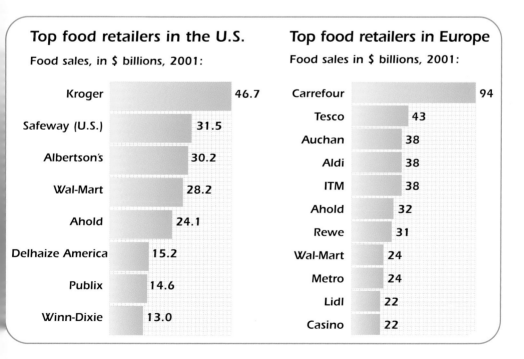

Top food retailers in the U.S.

Food sales, in $ billions, 2001:

Kroger	46.7
Safeway (U.S.)	31.5
Albertson's	30.2
Wal-Mart	28.2
Ahold	24.1
Delhaize America	15.2
Publix	14.6
Winn-Dixie	13.0

Top food retailers in Europe

Food sales in $ billions, 2001:

Carrefour	94
Tesco	43
Auchan	38
Aldi	38
ITM	38
Ahold	32
Rewe	31
Wal-Mart	24
Metro	24
Lidl	22
Casino	22

EXPANSION ABROAD

Many supermarket chains have expanded overseas to open new stores in other countries. Sometimes they move to wealthy countries, such as when the U.S.-based Wal-Mart chain expanded into the United Kingdom in 1999 by buying UK supermarket chain Asda. Supermarket chains also try to break into new territories, as when UK-based Tesco tried to expand into Malaysia. The Malaysian government felt that Tesco would have a negative effect on local businesses, and tried to stop the company from building stores there.

SUPERMARKET CHAINS AND INTERNATIONAL TRADE

Supermarkets buy foods from all over the world. Trade in food (the shipping and buying and selling before the food is sold to a consumer) has grown much more than food production over the last few decades. Imagine you sell a cow today at market. First it is shipped to eastern England, and bought at another market by a Dutch company. Then it is sent to Holland where a wholesaler butchers it, sells it to several local businesses and finally, they sell it to consumers. That is five transactions, as opposed to selling a cow to a butcher who sells it to a customer, which is only two transactions.

Supermarkets decide where to buy food based largely on where it is cheapest. If it is cheaper for a European Supermarket to buy rice in Thailand than Turkey, that is where they buy it. Supermarkets say that this is because their customers are most interested in the cost of food, not where it comes from. However, having realized that people will pay extra for especially tasty food, or for organic food (see pages 26 and 27), most supermarkets now stock these at higher prices.

A supermarket representative meets with a local fruit grower. Supermarkets have been criticized for their treatment of suppliers. Some people argue that supermarkets are only motivated by buying at the lowest possible price in order to make the highest possible profit.

Wal-Mart's global expansion

The U.S.-based Wal-Mart company has over 3,500 stores in the United States. In 1991, it started to expand into other territories; by 2002, it planned to spend $9.2 billion on worldwide expansion.

Country	Year of Wal-Mart entry	Number of stores
Mexico	1991	551
Puerto Rico	1992	17
Canada	1994	196
Brazil	1995	23
Argentina	1995	11
China	1995	19
South Korea	1998	9
Germany	1998	95
United Kingdom	1999	250

Food and trade

This chart shows the increase in the amount of particular types of food produced, as well as the increase in the percentage of foods traded internationally.

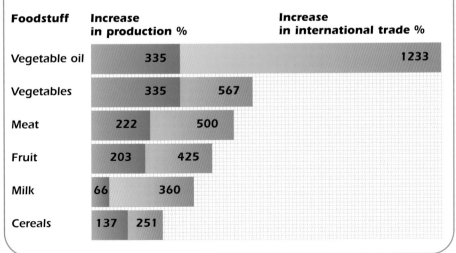

Foodstuff	Increase in production %	Increase in international trade %
Vegetable oil	335	1233
Vegetables	335	567
Meat	222	500
Fruit	203	425
Milk	66	360
Cereals	137	251

Demonstrators protest against the World Trade Organization, accusing it of unfair treatment of developing countries.

Trade barriers

Sometimes a country or group of countries decide to create trade barriers. These are ways of keeping goods from being imported from elsewhere. For example, imagine the Czech Republic traditionally makes and sells wooden toys. Then makers of wooden toys from South Africa begin to sell their goods in the Czech Republic. Because the cost of making them is lower in South Africa, the toys are cheaper. Fewer Czech-made toys are sold as a result. So the Czech government creates a new tax to be charged on all imported wooden toys. Suddenly the South African toys are more expensive because the import tax is added to their cost.

In the same way, countries have tried in the past to protect their food producers from foreign competition. Trade barriers such as these still exist between different trading groups, such as the European Union or the North American Free Trade Association. Within these groups there are not supposed to be barriers to trade between the member countries. But there are controls on goods that can be imported from outside the group.

Subsidies

Countries and groups of countries also try to help their food producers through **subsidies**. These are payments made to food producers by the government—for example, wheat farmers in the midwestern United States, or dairy farmers in Germany—to help them stay in business.

Environmental stewardship

In some areas, such as the United Kingdom, farmers are paid money for looking after the land (called environmental stewardship). This is instead of receiving subsidies for producing food. The goals of this program are to improve the countryside and to stop supermarket chains from adjusting the prices they pay according to the subsidies that are available to farmers.

The World Trade Organization

The World Trade Organization (WTO) is an international body that tries to promote trade between nations. There are 148 member countries who agree to follow its rules. The WTO helps its members make trade agreements, and acts as a court for countries that get into disputes about trade.

The WTO has been criticized in the past for several reasons. Some people argue that wealthy countries dominate and tend to set the rules to suit themselves. Because members have to agree to follow the WTO's decisions, it can be impossible for poorer countries to get decisions made in their interests. People also argue that the WTO does not do enough to protect workers in poorer countries.

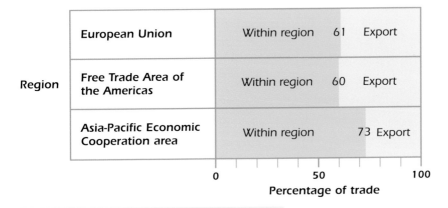

This chart shows how much trade goes on within three of the world's biggest trading areas, compared to their total exports out of the areas.

Technology and food

Today, **crop yields** (the amount of a crop that can be grown on an area of land) and the numbers of animals that can be raised on a given area of land are higher than ever before. Technology allows farmers to increase the productivity of their land using developments in farming techniques, chemical treatments of crops, and even genetic engineering.

Chemical pesticides are often sprayed onto crops from airplanes in order to efficiently cover large fields.

Farming and chemicals

One of the biggest changes in agriculture since the 1940s has been the increase in factory farming. At factory farms animals are reared in limited space and fattened up as quickly as possible to be ready for sale. Their feed, which is usually grain such as corn, sorghum, or soybean meal, is mixed with vitamins and minerals. Some farmers also add chemicals to speed growth, and **antibiotics** to prevent illness. As soon as they reach the required size, the animals are sent away for slaughter.

Arable farmers use chemicals to control pests that might attack their crops or to add **nutrients** to the soil. Sometimes these chemicals are no longer used in wealthy countries because they are dangerous, but they are still used in poorer countries. One example of this is the pesticide DDT, which is banned in the United States and Europe but is still used elsewhere in the world.

Food additives

Chemicals are also added to food that is processed before sale. Sugar and salt are often added to food to make it tastier, and other chemicals are added to keep it fresh. In 2000, the food industry spent an estimated $20 billion on such additives, and in richer countries people eat an average of 14 pounds (6.5 kilograms) of additives a year. Often it is the cheapest foods, usually bought by the poorest people in wealthy countries, that contain the most additives.

GM crops

GM stands for genetically modified. GM crops have had their genetic material altered by scientists, to make them grow faster, be more resistant to disease, or have other desirable qualities. GM crops are controversial, however; find out more on pages 38 and 39.

Golden Rice

Some people consider Golden Rice to be an example of how GM crops can help poorer countries keep people healthy. In Asia, rice is a major part of many people's diet. However, rice is low in **beta-carotene**, and many people lack this vitamin in their diets. A lack of beta-carotene can lead to blindness and sometimes death.

Golden Rice has been genetically altered to increase the amount of beta-carotene it contains. It is hoped that this will lead to improvements in people's health.

Organic food

Organic food first became popular among people who were concerned about the amount of chemicals and pesticides used on the food they ate, as well as the effect of the food industry on the environment. Exact rules about what makes food organic differ from country to country. In general, though, organic farmers do not use chemical pesticides and fertilizers on plants, or antibiotics and **growth hormones** on animals. They also do not grow GM crops.

Increasing amounts of land are being classified as organic, especially in richer countries. Normally land has to go through a specific process to be classified as organic. This process takes several years, during which only organic practices can be followed. Organic farmers also usually try to conserve resources, land, and water as much as possible. Most farmers in poorer countries already farm their land organically. Roughly 80 percent would not need to change their farming techniques to be registered as organic.

WHY IS ORGANIC FOOD POPULAR?

Globally, the sales of organic food have grown 20 percent a year since the early 1990s. In 2002, sales reached $23 billion. Organic food has become popular for several reasons:

- people feel that food grown without chemicals and additives is healthier
- food that is bought locally, rather than being transported long distances, is responsible for less pollution
- farmers can get better prices by selling their crops directly to consumers, helping them offset the added costs of growing food organically
- many people believe that organic food tastes better.

ORGANIC FOOD SUPPLY

Organic food was originally sold close to where it was grown since this cut down on the environmental impact of transporting it. Farmers would bring their crops to a local farmers' market or rely on door-to-door delivery, where one vehicle delivered food directly to customers.

Today, not all organic food is grown locally. Instead, organizations such as supermarkets import it. According to the U.S. Department of Agriculture, the United States imported between $1 billion and $1.5 billion in organic food in 2002, roughly 11 percent of what it spent on organic food. In the United Kingdom, about 70 percent of organic food is now imported. The environmental benefits of selling food close to where it is grown are now being lost, even in the organic market.

What can you do?

If you want to support the organic food industry's goals:

- buy local, rather than imported, organic food
- buy food from farmers' markets
- don't drive to buy your food: go by bicycle or bus.

Impacts of the Food Industry

The food that is available for us to buy, and what we choose to eat, has a major effect on our lives.

Food in richer countries

In the world's richer countries, people tend to leave home in the morning for work and return in the early evening. They arrive back home tired and many do not want to cook meals from scratch. As a result, there has been a huge growth in frozen foods or frozen dinners. These are packaged meals that simply need to be heated up before being eaten.

Frozen foods or frozen dinners bring with them potential problems. They are typically (though not always) high in protein, fats, and sugar, and often lack **fiber** and carbohydrates. **Nutritionists** say that a diet made up of such foods is not as healthy as a more balanced diet including fresh foods.

Packaged food is especially popular among city dwellers, who are now the fastest-growing part of the world's population.

PROCESSED FOODS

Processed foods have been prepared for sale to make them easier for the consumer to use. At the simplest level, this means that basic tasks have been completed before the food is bought: for example, 90 percent of the chicken sold in the United States has already been **deboned**. More complicated processed food includes such items as breakfast cereal, washed and mixed salads, and specially prepared dishes.

In 1996, Britain decided to slaughter 100,000 cattle as a result of an outbreak of BSE.

Processed food may have chemicals and sometimes extras added to it, often without this being clearly marked on the packaging. In many countries this is no longer allowed. The UK-based Tesco group, for example, was fined in 2002 for selling pork without declaring on the labeling that water, glucose syrup, and salt had been added to the meat.

PUBLIC HEALTH

One of the major food issues in richer countries is public health, especially obesity. An increasing number of people are obese, which can lead to a variety of health difficulties, including problems with joints, heart problems, circulatory problems, and diabetes. The costs of caring for people with obesity-related health problems are likely to rise as more people are affected.

A second food-related public health issue has to do with the spread of diseases such as BSE (Bovine Spongiform Encephalopathy), otherwise known as mad-cow disease. People feared that the meat from cows with this disease could pass on the human form of BSE, Creutzfeldt-Jakob disease. There were several cases reported in the United Kingdom in the 1990s. A single case of BSE in Canada caused the United States to temporarily close its borders to Canadian beef imports.

Food and the world's poorer countries

In theory, the international trade in food can benefit poorer countries. They can develop industries based on the export of particular crops. These provide new employment for local people. In addition, many poorer countries also have large foreign debts, and the income from selling food on the international market can help to pay these off.

However, the international trade in food sometimes brings economic disaster to poorer countries. There are two main reasons for this:

- Typically, foreign buyers are interested in a particular crop, such as coffee or cocoa. Land that had previously been used to grow food for local sale is turned over to production of only this crop. The poorer country may have to import basic foods that it used to grow itself.
- The poorer country also becomes dependent on the international price of the crop that it produces. Ethiopia, for example, receives 60 percent of its foreign earnings from the sale of coffee. Since the price of coffee has fallen by 70 percent since 1997, Ethiopia is worse off.

Changing diets

Although in some areas of poorer countries people often do not have enough food, in the cities there are other problems. Among people who can afford to eat well, diets are changing and becoming less healthy:

- people are eating less traditional foods, such as chickpeas and lentils
- they are eating more meat, fat, salt, and sugar
- processed and frozen foods are becoming increasingly popular
- people are drinking more alcohol
- people are eating less-varied diets.

Kenyan food exports

Between 1969 and 1999, Kenya doubled its vegetable production. At the same time, though, its exports of food increased by 6 times, from 11,000 tons in 1969 to 67,000 tons in 1999. The effect was that fewer vegetables were available to Kenyans themselves: in 1969 an average Kenyan ate 55 pounds (24.9 kilograms) of vegetables, but by 1999 this had dropped to 40 pounds (18.1 kilograms).

Most of Kenya's vegetable exports go to the United Kingdom. Between 70 and 90 percent of African food exports to the United Kingdom are controlled by supermarkets, who take 45 percent of the sales price. Although more farming jobs are created (left), farmers receive only about 17 percent of the sales price.

Debates About Food

We all have to eat in order to live. But which foods we choose to eat have important effects on our health and on the world's environment. The foods people in richer countries choose to eat also affect the lifestyles of people in poorer countries. Our food choices also raise concerns about animal welfare within the food industry.

Food advertising

The food industry spends roughly $40 billion each year persuading us to buy food. Fresh foods in general are rarely advertised, but **branded, processed foods** or giant food chains are often advertised. Processed foods are normally less healthy than non-processed foods.

Governments and international organizations try to encourage people to eat healthier foods. But their efforts are often dwarfed by the campaigns of the food industry. For example, for every dollar spent by the World Health Organization on trying to improve the world's nutrition, $500 is spent on advertising by the food industry.

Food advertising is heaviest in richer countries. In 1999, Coca-Cola, for example, spent $1.22 per person on advertising in the United States; in Romania, although ads cost less, it spent just 20 cents per person.

Young customers

Around the world, increasing numbers of children are obese. Some observers suggest that the food advertising industry is partly responsible. Investigations have discovered that advertisers go to amazing lengths to attract children without their parents' knowledge. In particular, they use viral marketing—non-traditional advertising methods that do not appear to be ads at all. These ads can be found in children's websites, TV shows, and concerts to get across the "secret message" of how "cool" certain foods are, however unhealthy they may be.

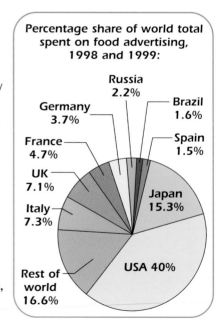

Percentage share of world total spent on food advertising, 1998 and 1999:

Russia 2.2%
Brazil 1.6%
Germany 3.7%
France 4.7%
Spain 1.5%
UK 7.1%
Japan 15.3%
Italy 7.3%
USA 40%
Rest of world 16.6%

Food education fails

In 2004, two separate European studies discovered that, although children were being taught about healthy eating in school, they were not choosing to eat healthy foods. Only six percent, for example, chose a salad or fresh vegetable at lunchtime. This might help to explain why one in six children under the age of fifteen were obese.

Fair Trade

Farmers in poorer countries receive only a relatively small amount of the money that is paid in wealthy countries for food they have grown. The rest is paid to transportation companies, food processors, distributors, and supermarkets. To make matters worse, while the prices paid for crops such as tea, coffee, and sugar have stayed the same, the prices farmers in poorer countries have to pay for machinery, fertilizers, and pesticides have all increased.

Among the most popular Fair Trade products are tea and coffee. Here, a tea plantation worker in India gathers tea leaves.

To try to change this situation, Fair Trade organizations agree to buy food from farmers in poorer countries at a pre-set price. The price is usually higher than the farmers could get elsewhere, and often it includes what is called a social premium. This is a part of the payment that is meant to pay for social or environmental improvements. For example, in Ghana some Fair Trade crops are weeded by hand, which means that harmful pesticides do not have to be used. The social premium pays for the extra work required by hand weeding.

In Europe alone, sales of Fair Trade goods were more than $550 million in 2001–2002. Worldwide, sales of Fair Trade coffee have grown from 11,000 tons in 1995 to 15,000 tons in 2001. Brewing up the largest pots were Germany and the Netherlands (where the first Fair Trade labeling began in 1989), where consumers drank 3,300 tons of Fair Trade coffee.

Animal transportation

Each year, roughly 44 million cows, sheep, and pigs are traded internationally. Millions more are traded across long distances in large countries such as the United States. For example, Australia exports five million live sheep each year to the Middle East. The sheep face a long journey to port in Australia, then a two- to three-week sea voyage before they reach their destination.

Some animal rights supporters feel that this international trade in live animals is cruel and unnecessary. They argue that it creates profit from the suffering of animals and should be banned. However, animal export is big business, and employs thousands of people around the world. In Australia alone, the industry was worth $127 million in 2000.

Before they are slaughtered, sheep are often transported in cramped feeding pens.

The environment

PESTICIDES

Pesticides are chemicals used to prevent damage to crops, mainly by weeds, insects, and fungi. They allow farmers to increase the amount of food they can grow on their land, and have resulted in fewer workers needed for jobs such as weeding.

Four of the largest companies together sold over $15 billion of pesticides in 1999. Between 1980 and 1999, worldwide sales of pesticides grew from $11.7 million to $30.2 million. Much of the increase in sales was to poorer countries, where farmers have begun to develop **intensive agriculture**, producing food for sale abroad. The chemicals themselves are expensive for farmers in poorer countries to buy, though the farmers hope to make more money from their crops by using them. But there are other costs to pesticide use:

- The long-term effects of pesticides kill thousands of people each year, almost all of them in poorer countries. There, farmers may not be fully aware of the dangers in using these chemicals.
- Pesticides affect the environment. They poison animals and get into water supplies, which can affect the health of local people.
- When pesticides are used, they sometimes kill creatures that would naturally prey on the pests. This means that if pests reappear, even more pesticide may be necessary to kill the new pests.

Farm workers in developed countries have to wear protective clothing when dealing with pesticides.

GM CROPS

GM (genetically modified) crops have had their genetic structure changed by scientists to make them grow bigger, be more resistant to disease, or have other desirable characteristics. The first GM plant was a type of tobacco. It was produced in 1983. In the next 20 years, over 60 species were genetically modified. Among these are plants from all the major food groups along with trees, cattle, sheep, fish, and insects.

Genetic engineering allows scientists to move genes from one species to another. Usually, this is done by taking a desirable gene from one type of plant and moving it to another. The same is true of GM animals, where, for example, the genes that encourage fast growth in one type of cattle could be added to another. Even more radical modifications are possible. Genes from fish that have resistance to cold have been transferred into some strawberries, for example, to see if they help the strawberries withstand cold temperatures.

Dolly the sheep, seen here with her own lamb, was a genetically modified animal. Her genetic makeup was identical to that of another sheep. She was the first animal cloned from a single-parent animal.

The spread of GM

The first commercial GM crops were grown in the United States in 1996.
By 2001 the United States had over 88 million acres of GM cropland. Today,
U.S. farmers grow GM corn, cotton, canola, and soybeans. Argentina, China,
Canada, Australia, and South Africa also have significant areas where GM
crops are grown. Worldwide, GM areas grew from 27 million acres in 1997
to 130 million acres in 2001.

PROTECTING THE INVESTMENT

Large companies have spent huge amounts of money developing these
crops, and as a result they have taken out **patents** to make sure other
people cannot use them without paying the company. In 2003, there were
already 2,181 patents on corn, and 1,110 patents on potatoes. In addition,
some GM crops will not grow unless a specific chemical, available from the
company that developed the crop, is used on them.

*Demonstrators stage a protest
in a field of GM crops. Many
people are concerned about
the effects of the spread of
GM foods.*

ANTI-GM CAMPAIGNS

Many people do not want to eat GM food. In Europe, for example, food producers and processors have been forced to use non-GM ingredients. In 2003, no European country had more than 250,000 acres of land being used to grow GM food. Many ordinary people are worried about the long-term effects of GM crops on their health. For example, some GM plants contain antibiotic genes. People worry that this might mean diseases will become increasingly resistant to antibiotics.

Critics of GM foods say that companies should not be allowed to patent a type of food crop. They also point out that the extra costs involved in buying GM seeds and chemicals may mean that poorer farmers end up in debt. Finally, environmental campaigners believe that GM crops would harm the natural environment if they "escape" and grow where they are not wanted.

For and against GM foods

For:	Against:
GM crops are more productive and will help feed the world's growing population.	Development of GM crops is aimed at making a profit, not helping the poor.
GM crops can be grown where ordinary crops cannot grow effectively, making more farmland available.	Farmers will end up being dependent on GM companies for their seeds and other chemicals.
GM crops can be engineered to contain extra nutrients.	GM crops, designed to be tougher than normal crops, might spread and grow where they are not wanted. Eventually this could make it impossible to eat non-GM food.
Vaccines (things that stimulate resistance to disease) can be produced cheaply in GM plants.	

Tomorrow's Table

Food buyers in wealthy countries are faced with a bewildering variety of choices. A typical supermarket might stock 20 different types of chicken, 100 different kinds of potato chips, and 7 different types of baked beans. Some will be labeled "low-fat," others "extra-tasty," and still others are "best value." Foods today are supposed to be labeled to show what they contain, but many people do not fully understand the meaning of the labels.

Food labeling also cannot show the processes that food has gone through before being sold. Some salami, for example, is dusted with flour to make it look more rustic (and tastier) than it is. The flour itself may have been bleached with chlorine or chlorine-dioxide to make it look whiter. "Mature" cheese may have had acid added to it to make it tastier.

Tricks of the trade

Large food retailers have developed several practices that many people are unaware of:
- "fresh" meat is injected with additives and water
- food is sealed in packages from which oxygen (which ages foods) has been removed; tests have shown that this might reduce the vitamins the food contains
- salads are washed in water containing twenty times as much chlorine as would be put into swimming-pool water
- sandwiches and pre-prepared meals contain far more salt than the recommended healthy level.

Consumer choice

Faced with this situation, increasing numbers of people are choosing to eat differently. For example, they opt for organic foods, which they know have been grown and prepared for sale in a particular way. Bread machines, for baking bread at home, have become increasingly popular. People everywhere are becoming more aware of what they eat as well as food's effect on their health and on the wider world.

Daily bread

An estimated 84 percent of all bread sold in the United States—$13.5 billion worth—is sold in supermarkets. In 2004, reports revealed that much of the bread sold in supermarkets contained large amounts of fat. Just three slices of some bread had more fat than a typical candy bar. One loaf had 0.3 ounces (8.8 grams) of fat in every 3.5 ounces (100 grams) of bread.

When fat is added to bread, it allows the bread to be made with a larger amount of air and water. The fat also keeps the bread fresh for longer. The fat used in this way is hydrogenated fat. A Harvard University study revealed that hydrogenated fats are directly linked to heart disease, cancer, and obesity.

Statistical Information

Water

As well as food, we all need water to stay alive. By 2025, it is estimated that two-thirds of the world's population will be short of water.

Average annual domestic water use in 2000, in gallons per person

Gambia	260
Cambodia	430
Kenya	3,400
China	5,300
Netherlands	6,600
United Kingdom	10,600
Malaysia	16,000
Brazil	18,000
Russia	25,900
France	26,900
United States	56,800
Australia	131,000

The cost of keeping clean

One flush of the toilet (average)	2.6 gals.
Showering	9.2 gals.
Using dishwasher	9.2 gals.
Bathing	21.1 gals.

Water consumption as percentage of global water use

Agricultural	73 percent
Industrial	18 percent
Domestic	9 percent

Food and health

A balanced diet, including fruit and vegetables, is considered important for people to remain in good health.

Amount of vegetables consumed every day by each person over 29 years old:

United Kingdom, Israel, Spain, France	15.8oz (450g)
Australia	14.4oz (410g)
Algeria, Sierra Leone	12.3oz (350g)
China, Malaysia, Fiji	11.6oz (330g)
United States and Canada	10.2oz (290g)
India, Bangladesh	8.4oz (240g)
Mexico	6.7oz (190g)

Average body mass index (BMI) for adults over 29 years old (a BMI of between 20 and 25 is considered healthy)

United States and Canada	26.9
United Kingdom, Israel, Spain, France	26.7
Mexico	26
Australia	23.4
China, Malaysia, Fiji	22.9
Algeria, Sierra Leone	21.3
India, Bangladesh	19.9

Life expectancy in years, in 2000

Australia	78.7
Canada	78.5
Israel	78.3
France	78.1
Spain	78.1
United Kingdom	77.2
United States	76.5
Mexico	72.2
Malaysia	71.9
China	69.8
Algeria	68.9
Fiji	68.4
India	62.3
Bangladesh	58.1
Sierra Leone	37.3

Average daily calorie intake per person, in 1997

United States	3,699
France	3,518
Spain	3,310
Israel	3,278
United Kingdom	3,276
Australia	3,224
Canada	3,119
Mexico	3,097
Malaysia	2,977
China	2,897
Fiji	2,865
Algeria	2,853
India	2,496
Bangladesh	2,086
Sierra Leone	2,035

Glossary

Agricultural Revolution period of time in the 1700s and 1800s when there were many developments in farming in Europe and North America

antibiotic drug used by doctors to fight infectious bacterial diseases

arable land that is capable of growing crops. An arable farm is one on which crops are grown.

beta-carotene vitamin necessary for good health

branded a branded product is one that is available under a specific name, such as Burger King burgers or a Coca-Cola drink

calorie measure of the energy contained in food

carbohydrate type of nutrient in food

consumer person who buys and uses a product

cotton gin device for separating cotton fiber from the seeds

crop yield amount of a crop that can be raised from a given area of land. Crop yields are often increased using fertilizers.

deboned having the bones removed, such as from a piece of meat

diabetes disease that affects the body's blood supply, mainly by reducing its ability to process glucose (a type of sugar) contained in blood

efficient working well without losing much energy

environment surroundings

fat type of nutrient in food

fertilizer something added to soil to help grow crops

fiber part of food that helps our digestion work properly

genetically modified (GM) describes an organism that has had its genetic material altered

greenhouse gases gases such as carbon dioxide that some believe contribute to global warming (the gradual rise in Earth's average temperature). These gases trap heat inside the atmosphere.

growth hormone chemical that increases size and growth rates

intensive agriculture type of agriculture that tries to make the land as productive as possible, often by using fertilizers and pesticides

irrigation use of water to grow crops

malnutrition/malnourished lacking food with enough nutrients

mechanized work done by machinery rather than people or animals

mineral substance formed naturally in rocks and earth

nutrient substance required for staying alive. These include the minerals that plants take from the soil, and the parts of food that the human body needs in order to grow and remain healthy.

nutritionist person who gives advice on food and its effect on health

obese when a person's weight is more than 20 percent over their ideal weight, and affects their health

patent legal device that guarantees an inventor the "ownership" of their invention

pesticide chemical used to kill pests, especially insects

productivity rate at which a product is produced, as well as the amount that is produced

protein substance found in some foods that living things need to grow new cells and replace old ones

seed drill machine for planting seeds quickly and cheaply

subsidy financial help given by the government

subsistence means of supporting life

supermarket large store that stocks food and other products in large quantities

under-nutrition/undernourished/ under-nourishment lacking food

urbanized more like a city or town than like the countryside

vitamin chemical that the body needs to stay healthy

watchdog someone responsible for making sure people are treated fairly

Further Reading

Books

Paladio, Catherine. *One Good Apple: Growing Our Food for the Sake of the Earth*. Boston: Houghton Mifflin, 2000.

This book discusses the problems caused by pesticides, and also explains the benefits of organic farming.

Ridgewell, Jenny. *Examining Food and Nutrition*. Chicago: Heinemann Educational, 1996.

This title gives a good overview of food issues.

Tull, Anita. *Food and Nutrition*. New York: Oxford University Press, 1997.

Ask an adult to look at the following books with you:

Critser, Greg. *Fat Land: How Americans Became the Fattest People in the World*. New York: Houghton Mifflin, 2003.
This title has some fascinating information about obesity.

Millstone, Erik, and Lang, Tim. *The Atlas of Food: Who Eats What, Where and Why*. New York: Penguin, 2003.
This is a sister publication to *The State of the World Atlas* (see below). It is an equally useful book that provides information on almost every aspect of food, the food industry, and health issues associated with it.

Nestle, Marion. *Food Politics: How the Food Industry Influences Nutrition and Health*. Los Angeles: University of California Press, 2003.
This title contains some useful information on the food industry.

Smith, Dan. *The State of the World Atlas*. New York: Penguin, 2003.
This map-based graphic presentation of facts and figures under such headings as Power, Cost of Living, Rights, War and Force, Money, and Life and Death is invaluable. The book provides comparisons between different parts of the world, interesting statistics, and is regularly updated.

Websites

Oxfam International
www.oxfam.org
Oxfam is one of the oldest organizations campaigning and working against poverty. Follow the links to visit their country sites around the world.

ActionAid
www.actionaid.org
Working in over 30 countries, with more than 6 million of the world's poorest people, ActionAid is dedicated to creating a world without poverty where everyone has enough to eat. 'Actionzone' is a special link for young people.

United States Agency for International Development (USAID)
www.usaid.gov
USAID is the United States' main provider of aid and food assistance overseas.

Soil Association
www.soilassociation.org
This website has advice on organic food, including a useful "Library" section full of articles, research papers, and press releases.

Index